# zendoodle coloring

# Panda Playtime

*Cuddly Cubs to Color and Display*

*illustrations by*
## Jeanette Wummel

### CASTLE POINT BOOKS
NEW YORK

ZENDOODLE COLORING: PANDA PLAYTIME.
Copyright © 2022 by St. Martin's Press. All rights reserved.
Printed in the United States of America. For information, address
St. Martin's Publishing Group, 120 Broadway, New York, NY 10271.

www.castlepointbooks.com

The Castle Point Books trademark is owned by Castle Point Publishing, LLC.
Castle Point books are published and distributed by St. Martin's Publishing Group.

ISBN 978-1-250-27976-7 (trade paperback)

Our books may be purchased in bulk for promotional, educational, or business use.
Please contact your local bookseller or the Macmillan Corporate and Premium
Sales Department at 1-800-221-7945, extension 5442, or by email
at MacmillanSpecialMarkets@macmillan.com.

First Edition: 2022

10 9 8 7 6 5 4 3 2 1

# zendoodle coloring

## Panda Playtime

Other great books in the series
# zendoodle coloring